TIGER WOODS

GOLF'S SHINING YOUNG STAR

BY BILL GUTMAN

MILLBROOK SPORTS WORLD
THE MILLBROOK PRESS
BROOKFIELD, CONNECTICUT

Photographs courtesy of Focus on Sports: cover; Allsport: cover inset (© David Cannon), pp. 3 (© J. D. Cuban), 13 (© Ken Levine), 14-15 (© Alan D. Levenson), 17 (© Gary Newkirk), 31 (© J. D. Cuban), 32 (© J. D. Cuban); AP/Wide World Photos: pp. 4, 21, 24, 26, 28, 35, 38, 42; © David Strick/Outline: pp. 9, 10; Seth Poppel Yearbook Archives: p. 19; © Reuters/Archive Photos: pp. 23 (Conan D. Owen), 40 (Apichart Weerawong), 43 (John Kuntz), 44 (Mike Blake), 46 (Gary Hershorn).

Library of Congress Cataloging-in-Publication Data
Gutman, Bill.
Tiger Woods : golf's shining young star / Bill Gutman.
p. cm. — (Millbrook sports world)
Includes index.
Summary: A biography of the youngest golfer to win the Masters Tournament, from his childhood in California to his development as one of the most highly recognized players of the game.
ISBN 0-7613-0309-X (lib. bdg.). — ISBN 0-7613-0329-4 (pbk.)
1. Woods, Tiger—Juvenile literature. 2. Golfers—United States—Biography—Juvenile literature. [1. Woods, Tiger. 2. Golfers. 3. Racially mixed people—Biography.] I. Title. II. Series.
GV964.W66G88 1998
796.352'092—dc21
[B] 97-25906 CIP AC

Published by The Millbrook Press, Inc.
2 Old New Milford Road
Brookfield, Connecticut 06804

Printed in the United States of America
5 4 3 2

Tiger Woods

In August 1996, twenty-year-old Eldrick "Tiger" Woods stepped onto the Pumpkin Ridge Golf Course near Portland, Oregon, with a chance to make history. Though he had just recently completed his sophomore year at Stanford University, the 6-foot-2-inch (188-centimeter), 155-pound (70-kilogram) Woods was trying to become the first golfer ever to win three straight United States Amateur championships. Amateur tournaments are for players who have not yet turned professional. They do not get paid or win prize money.

After two rounds of medal play (thirty-six holes), Tiger Woods had a 69 and a 67 for a total of 136. That was the best of all the golfers. Now, he and sixty-three others began match play. That meant that they played directly against each other. Total score didn't count. The winner would be the one who had the best score on more holes.

It was this kind of grim determination that enabled Tiger Woods to win a third straight United States Amateur golf championship. To do it, Tiger had to come from behind and win in a sudden-death playoff.

Tiger ripped through his early opponents easily. When he reached the semi-final, he defeated his Stanford teammate, Joel Kribel, 3 and 1. That meant that Tiger had won three more holes than Kribel with just one hole left. So the match ended because there was no way Kribel could win.

Now came the final. Tiger would be going up against Steve Scott, a good golfer who was just nineteen years old. The two golfers would play two full rounds of match play, thirty-six holes, to determine the champion. At first, it looked like Scott's day. He was four holes ahead of Tiger by the time they had played the first nine holes.

Scott continued to play well, while Tiger struggled. With just sixteen holes remaining, Scott had a five-hole lead. But those who were watching knew that the match wasn't over yet. Anyone who had followed Tiger's remarkable career knew that he could never be counted out. He always seemed to play his best when the chips were down.

And suddenly, he began to do it again.

Tiger began his comeback by winning three straight holes, starting with the twenty-first. But Scott wouldn't quit, not even after Tiger made an amazing 45-foot (14-meter) putt on the twenty-ninth hole. With three holes left, Steve Scott still was 2 up. He had won two more holes than Tiger.

Once again Tiger Woods dug down deep inside himself. He had a tremendous will to win. During the tournament he was asked if he thought he had the most mental toughness of anyone in the field. He calmly said, "Yes, I do."

Now he would need all of that mental toughness. He won the thirty-fourth hole to pull within one. On the thirty-fifth, he sank an incredible 35-foot (11-meter) putt to win the hole and tie the match.

It was still tied after the thirty-sixth hole, and the two golfers had to go to a sudden-death play-off. That meant that the first one to win a hole would win the championship. Neither golfer won the thirty-seventh hole, the first of sudden death. Now came the thirty-eighth. It was a short hole, just 194 yards (177 meters) long and a par 3 (meaning that a golfer should be able to complete the hole in three strokes).

Tiger hit his first shot to within 12 feet (4 meters) of the hole, or cup, as it is called. Scott's first shot went into the high grass alongside the green, and his second shot went 11 feet (3 meters) past the hole. Tiger's putt came within 18 inches (46 centimeters) of the cup. It was his second shot. Scott then missed his putt on his third shot. If Tiger could make his third shot, a short putt, he would win.

Tiger lined it up carefully. Then he stood over the ball and concentrated on the shot. He stroked it firmly, and it rolled in. With that, Tiger had won his third straight United States Amateur championship. No golfer had ever done that before. But Tiger Woods was already used to doing things no golfer had done before. He had picked up a golf club before he was a year old, and had been on a television show driving golf balls with legendary comedian Bob Hope when he was just two. And he had now won a national amateur championship in each of the last six years.

That wasn't all that made Tiger unique: One-fourth African American, one-fourth Chinese, one-fourth Thai, one-eighth American Indian, and one-eighth Caucasian, he had an unusual heritage. Because of his dark skin, he was generally perceived as a black man. Golf is a sport that has seen very few black players, although there have been a few good professional golfers who are black. But none of them became the golf superstar that Tiger was becoming.

Suddenly, there was a young man with an engaging smile who was a wizard with a golf club. He already had one of the most recognizable nicknames in sports. Many were predicting that he would take the golf world by storm. What they didn't realize is that he would also take the entire sporting world by storm.

A CHILDHOOD GEARED TO GOLF

When Eldrick “Tiger” Woods was born in Cypress, California, on December 30, 1975, his nickname and perhaps his whole future were planned out. Earl and Kultida “Tida” Woods lived in Cypress, located 35 miles (56 kilometers) southeast of Los Angeles, in a one-story tract house. Each had taken a long and sometimes dangerous road to get there.

Earl was a career army man who had a failed first marriage and three children he rarely saw. Though he was already in his mid-thirties, he wound up in the Green Berets doing two tours of duty in war-torn Vietnam. A lieutenant colonel, Earl was a natural leader who cheated death several times while in the war.

Earl and a South Vietnamese friend, Nguyen Phong, fought side by side in 1970 and saved each other’s lives. Earl called Phong “Tiger” because of his strength and will. Phong would later disappear, and Earl Woods never learned whether his friend was alive or dead. But he never forgot him, and nicknamed his son after him.

“I hoped my son would be as courageous as my friend,” Earl said. “I also hoped that someday, somehow, Phong would see the names Tiger and Woods together and make the connection.”

Earl met Kultida at the U.S. Army office in Bangkok, Thailand, in 1967. She was a native of Thailand and worked in the office as a secretary. She had grown up in a boarding school after her parents separated when she was five. The two married after Earl’s tour ended and went to the United States to live.

When their only son was born, Earl and Tida vowed to give him love, security, and a very solid upbringing. “We wanted him always to have the knowledge that there were two people whose lives were totally committed to him,” Earl Woods explained.

Shortly after Tiger was born, his father retired from the army and began working for the McDonnell Douglas Corporation. By that time one of his newfound passions was golf. Earl Woods played golf for the first time at age forty-two, two years before his son was born, after learning the sport from a book. The first time he played he shot an excellent 91 for seventeen holes.

When he was just eleven months old, Tiger was already playing golf and practicing on the putting green.

Earl continued to play golf after the birth of his son. When Tiger was just eleven months old, his father noticed how Tiger always looked at his golf clubs. So Earl sawed off one of the clubs and gave it to young Tiger. Sure enough, Tiger began to imitate his father's golf swing almost immediately.

That was just the beginning. Tiger simply took to the game from the start. He never had to be told to practice and never had to be pushed. If anything, his parents had to slow him down. It wasn't long before his father saw that his son had a chance to be someone very special. He was determined that young Tiger wouldn't be held back.

"I was a black kid, and golf was played at the country club—end of story," Earl said. "But I told myself that somehow my son would get a chance to play golf early in life." Earl Woods meant that when he was young, blacks were not allowed in many country clubs unless they worked there. He didn't want his son to be excluded that way. Earl began taking Tiger to the nearby Navy Golf Course (NGC). By the time Tiger was just two, he already played the game amazingly well. That's when his mother called Los Angeles sportscaster Jim Hill. Hill came to the NGC and filmed young Tiger playing one hole. He couldn't believe his eyes and ran his story on television.

At the age of three, Tiger had perfected a smooth swing that predicted future greatness.

A short time later, Tiger was on television once again. He appeared on *The Mike Douglas Show*, driving golf balls with legendary comedian Bob Hope. A few years later, Tiger appeared on the show *That's Incredible!*, showing his incredible golf talent at age five. But the best was yet to come.

LESSONS IN GOLF AND IN LIFE

Both Earl and Tida Woods were determined to give their son a complete education. To make him a good, productive person was their primary goal. They knew he would face certain hardships just because he was a child of mixed heritage with dark skin. They wanted him to have the character and strength to deal with those hardships.

It didn't take young Tiger long to experience racism. On his first day of kindergarten, a group of older kids grabbed him and tied him to a tree. They threw rocks at him and called him names like "monkey" and "nigger." Tiger was so upset that he didn't tell his parents for several days. But with this incident and others that followed, Earl Woods taught his son something else: He wanted him to always turn a negative into a positive.

"So many athletes who reach the top had things happen to them as children that created hostility," Mr. Woods said. "They bring that hostility with them. But that hostility uses up energy. If you can do it without the chip on the shoulder, it frees up all that energy to create."

Once young Tiger really began to show his ability as a golfer, his parents told him to always hold his tongue, follow the rules, and win; to always stay positive about himself and his talent.

Tiger's talent continued to amaze. His mother has photos of him putting on a practice green before he was one year old.

"When he was eighteen months old I would take him to the driving range at the Navy Golf Course," Tida Woods remembered. "When he was done hitting I would put him back in the stroller and he'd fall asleep."

When Tiger was four, his father began taking him to the Heartwell Park Golf Club where the club pro, Rudy Duran, wondered if Tiger was too young. As soon as he watched the little boy hit seven shots, however, he changed his mind.

"I saw a kid who popped out of the womb like a Magic Johnson or a Wolfgang Amadeus Mozart. He had talent oozing out of his fingertips."

Duran coached Tiger from the time he was four until he was ten. By that time Tiger loved golf more than anything else and was already beginning to win junior age-group tournaments. His parents knew then that he could have a great future in the game. But they also wanted to be sure that he learned other kinds of lessons, away from the golf course.

"Once Tiger reached school age there was no golf practice until his homework was done," Tida said. "He used to tell his friends that his mother was very strict."

She also used to tell him not to throw temper tantrums when he played. She didn't want him acting like a brat.

"I'd tell him I didn't want him to ruin my reputation as a parent," his mother said. "And I promised to spank him the minute he acted like that."

When Tiger was just four his father took him to participate in a nearby tournament. As he got out of the car, Earl Woods asked his son if he had put his clubs in the trunk; it was Tiger's responsibility to remember those things.

"Tiger had forgotten," Mr. Woods said. "He was trying to keep from crying. I made him wait about five minutes, then asked him if he had learned his lesson. He said he had. Only then did I take his clubs out from under the backseat. I hid them there when I realized he had forgotten them. I never had to worry about that again."

People who watched Tiger grow and develop say that his parents never pushed him to do anything. He simply took to golf. Jay Brunza, a retired captain and psychologist in the Navy Medical Service Corps, began playing golf with Tiger and his father when Tiger was entering his teen years. He soon became the young golfer's personal sports psychologist, working on relaxation, focusing, and anger management.

Golf was always a great joy for Tiger. Even in his early teen years his parents never had to force him to play. More often than not, there was a smile on his face, especially when he was playing well.

"Tiger was pursuing something from an intrinsic passion for the game," Brunza said. "He wasn't forced to live out somebody else's expectations. If he had said, 'I'm tired of golf, I want to collect stamps,' his parents would have said, 'Fine, son,' and would have walked him down to the post office."

Earl Woods also started to see his son's competitive drive. When Tiger was nine, his father began telling him to enjoy the game and to quit worrying about his scores and his numbers. Tiger replied quickly, "That's how I enjoy and am happy. I love shooting low numbers."

After that, Mr. Woods established custom-made pars for a golfer Tiger's age. If he felt Tiger should make a hole in six shots, that would be the par.

"By doing that, Tiger always felt he could compete," Mr. Woods said. "I didn't want him to have unrealistic expectations. That would be stupid of me."

All of these things helped Tiger to learn about responsibility. The lessons took hold. He never forgot them.

"[My parents] have raised me well," he would say later. "I truly believe they have taught me to accept full responsibility for all aspects of my life."

A CHAMPION IN THE MAKING

While Tiger Woods was considered a young golf wizard by the age of two, that didn't guarantee he'd be a champion later in life. Many things can happen to very gifted young children. Some are pushed too hard by their parents and then rebel. Others just lose interest. Still others burn out by their early teens and simply want to try something else.

As a teenager, Tiger improved his game rapidly. He practiced all the shots, including a chip. Notice how he keeps his head down even though he has already hit the ball. That's classic form.

None of these things happened to Tiger. From the time he swung that first sawed-off club before he was a year old, it was golf and nothing else. Tiger was a fine all-around athlete who had played football, baseball, basketball, and participated in track by his early teens, but he gave up these other sports, one by one, on his own. There were always coaches who wanted him to play, but Tiger said no. The reason was always the same. Other sports took too much time away from golf.

When Tiger was just eight years old he won his first junior world championship. He did it in the ten-and-under division, which meant that he was better than all the nine- and ten-year-olds, as well. And he did it in a way that would become his trademark—finishing very strong.

In that tournament, Tiger shot a five-under-par 49 in the final round at the par 3 (all holes are reasonably short and par 3, making the eighteen-hole course a par 54) Presidio Hills Golf Course in San Diego, California. From there, his legend grew.

By the time he was fourteen, Tiger had won five age-group world titles. That was two more than any other golfer his age had ever won. Those, added to his more than one hundred local junior titles, meant that there was hardly enough room for all his trophies in the Woods home. Tiger was a slim, dark-skinned youngster who could hit the ball a country mile. But he also had a good all-around game, as well as nerves of steel.

Notah Begay, his friend and fellow golfer, put it this way: "The other guys always asked me before a tournament if Tiger is really as good as people say he is. He had already taken on a celebrity status and most of the other guys were afraid of him [on the golf course]."

In August 1990, when he was still fourteen, Tiger played with twenty-one touring professionals (pros) in a round at the Insurance Golf Classic, a pro-junior event in Fort Worth, Texas. He amazed everyone by shooting a 69 for eighteen holes. That was good enough to beat or tie eighteen of the twenty-one professionals in the tournament.

Tiger's playing partner, a pro named Tommy Moore, said, "I wish I could have played like that at fourteen. Heck, I wish I could play like that at twenty-seven."

A year later Tiger was a freshman at Western High School in Anaheim, California. Yet he was already receiving recruiting letters from colleges with

In 1992, at the age of sixteen, Tiger became the youngest golfer ever to qualify for a PGA tour event. Still an amateur, he played in the Los Angeles Open against many top professionals. His natural talent amazed everyone.

top golf programs. The first of those letters had come from Stanford University when Tiger was just thirteen. Everyone who saw him play felt he had a bright future in golf. Even Tiger already had his own agenda.

"I plan to get my [college] degree first," he would say, "and then tear up the Tour [the pro golf tour]."

At fifteen, Tiger was 5 feet 11 inches (180 centimeters) and weighed just 138 pounds (63 kilograms). Golf took up a great deal of his time after his schoolwork. His father had retired from McDonnell Douglas and now traveled with his son. Jay Brunza also traveled with them.

"Tiger should not be portrayed as a Robo-Golfer," Brunza said. "He doesn't need motivation from anybody else. His motivation comes from within. I don't ever see him burning out, because golf is pure pleasure for him."

Tiger, however, was also increasingly aware of the burden he was carrying. There had been just a handful of black golfers on the pro Tour over the years. Men such as Calvin Peete, Lee Elder, Charlie Sifford, Jim Dent, Jim Thorpe, and Pete Brown had won a tournament occasionally. They were fine golfers, but they were not among the top stars of the game. When Tiger was fifteen he was told that a black golfer had not won a Professional Golf Association (PGA) Tour event in five years, since Peete had last won.

Because many golf courses were at private country clubs, and there were few public courses available to them, not many black or other minority youngsters played the game at an early age. In addition, the black pros had traditionally learned the game while caddying (carrying the clubs) for others.

Tiger had already heard more than once that he had a chance to blaze a trail for future generations. But he wanted to make one thing perfectly clear: "I don't want to be the best *black* golfer on the Tour," he said. "I want to be the best *golfer* on the Tour, period."

A handsome Tiger Woods graduated from Western High School in 1994. From there, he went on to Stanford University, where he was a fine student even as his golfing legend grew.

Before the year was over, fifteen-year-old Tiger Woods had won his first United States Junior Amateur championship. It was the start of a run that would bring him even more fame in the golf world and make people wonder all over again how this youngster had become so good so quickly.

His progress continued without a backward step. In 1993 he won his third straight United States Junior Amateur title, the first golfer ever to do so. He had just completed his junior year in high school. That summer he played in three PGA events, though he didn't come close to winning.

In the summer of 1994, Tiger graduated from Western High School with honors and had already signed a letter of intent to attend Stanford University in the fall on a full golf scholarship. But he had business to take care of first. Now that he was eighteen, he would be playing in his first United States Amateur championship against many golfers who were much older and more experienced.

None of that bothered Tiger. He ripped through the field and made it to the final round. There he would meet Trip Kuehne in a thirty-six-hole, match-play championship. Again, the pattern was familiar. After just thirteen holes, Kuehne had a six-hole lead and Tiger seemed to be in trouble. But that's when he made his move.

Suddenly, he was playing sensational golf, making one outstanding shot after another. When it was over, he and his father embraced. He had become the youngest United States Amateur champion ever.

That fall Tiger entered Stanford University in Stanford, California. He planned to major in economics and began studying hard, just as he had in high school. He enjoyed making new friends and still practiced golf as often as he could. During the summer following his freshman year he played in several PGA tournaments, including the Scottish Open in Scotland and the prestigious British Open (one of golf's four so-called major titles) at the famed St. Andrews Golf Course in England.

Though he didn't make the cut (a low enough score to continue on to the final two rounds), nineteen-year-old Tiger continued to learn. He watched how veteran pros controlled their shots in the wind at St. Andrews. His new coach, Butch Harmon, noticed how Tiger always watched other golfers intently, studying their every move.

"When he plays with guys like [Fred] Couples, [Greg] Norman, [Nick] Faldo, and [Nick] Price [all pro golf champions], he marvels at the way they control the ball in the air," Harmon said. "After the British Open, he said, 'Butch, how far away am I? When will I be that good?' I told him, 'You just have to keep working. You've still got so much to learn.'"

But he was learning fast. In late August 1995, he arrived at the Newport Country Club in Newport, Rhode Island, to defend his United States Amateur title. Once again, it wasn't easy. Tiger reached the semifinal where the match against Mark Plummer went down to the final hole. Tiger won it.

In the final, he was up against forty-three-year-old George "Buddy" Marucci. Once again, Tiger started slowly. But, as usual, he overcame his opponent's lead. When they came to the final hole of the match, Tiger was one up. He had to just tie or win the hole to take another championship.

But Marucci wasn't about to quit. His second shot put him on the green, the ball sitting just 20 feet (6 meters) from the cup. Tiger was 140 yards (128 meters) away. If he made a bad shot now, there was a good chance he would lose the hole. He picked out the club he wanted and stood over the ball, looking at the distant green.

In April 1995, Tiger played in his first Masters, as an amateur. Though he wasn't in contention, his youthful exuberance attracted large galleries. Here, he jumps in the air, hoping his ball won't carry into the gallery. It did, but he still birdied the hole.

Tiger took a short backswing and lofted the ball toward the cup. It flew over the flag (which marks the hole so it can be seen from a distance), hit the green, and its backspin took the ball to less than 1 foot (30 centimeters) from the hole. It was a brilliant shot.

Moments later, he made the short putt to win a second straight United States Amateur title, becoming the ninth player ever to win back-to-back titles in the ninety-five years the tournament had been held. Runner-up Marucci couldn't give enough praise to Tiger.

"He is the best athlete that this [level] of golf has seen," the older man said. "He's lean, he's strong, his swing is marvelous. I couldn't see the ball come off the club for the first twenty-seven holes. It came off the club that fast."

Jay Brunza saw yet another special quality in the budding young star. "Like all the great champions," Brunza said, "Tiger has the ability to raise his game when he has to."

As for Tiger, he was more than satisfied with his victory. "This one meant more [than the first Amateur title] because it showed how far my game has come. The shot at [hole number] eighteen. That was the only shot I could have hit that close. I didn't have it last year, but I do now."

During the post-tournament celebration, Earl Woods raised his glass in a toast to his son. "I'm going to make a prediction," he said. "Before he's through, my son will win fourteen major championships."

A THIRD STRAIGHT AND A BIG DECISION

Back at Stanford for his sophomore year, Tiger continued to point his life in one direction. He studied, practiced, and worked hard in the weight room. He wanted to build his strength without adding bulk to his body. Though he still appeared thin, he was quite strong and could hit the ball a long way.

He continued to play for Stanford, as well as in an occasional tournament when time permitted. He showed he was the cream of the college crop by winning the National Collegiate Athlete Association (NCAA) golf championship.

Once the school year ended he traveled to England to compete again in the British Open. Playing against the world's top professionals, Tiger was relaxed

Tiger played his first British Open in July 1995. Here, he enjoys a light moment with veteran professional Craig Stadler. Though Tiger still couldn't beat the pros, he took every opportunity to learn from them.

Tiger gives his trademark uppercut—his way of celebrating after sinking a long putt—during the 1996 U.S. Amateur championship. Tiger became the first golfer to win the title three years in a row.

and playing fine golf. In the second round, he stunned everyone by shooting a 66 to move up among the leaders. He actually had a chance to win the tournament.

"Something really clicked that day," Tiger said later. "I had found a whole new style of playing. I finally understood the meaning of playing within myself. After that, the game seemed a lot easier."

Tiger didn't win. But he finished in a tie for twenty-second place, his first top-twenty-five finish in a pro tournament. Now there was talk about when he would turn pro. Tiger began talking to touring pros: top golfers like Ernie Els, Curtis Strange, and Greg Norman. All of them told him basically the same thing. They felt he was ready for the pro Tour, both physically and mentally.

Tiger had always intended to get his college degree before turning pro. But now he wasn't sure he could wait another two years. The United States Amateur championship was coming up again. If he won it a third straight year, there would really be no other worlds for him to conquer as an amateur.

By the time Tiger arrived at Pumpkin Ridge for the 1996 United States Amateur championship the decision had been made. Tiger and those in his inner circle (his parents, coach, and friends) knew that he had decided to leave Stanford and turn professional. His coach, Butch Harmon, said it wouldn't be easy.

"All the amateur titles Tiger has won won't mean anything," Harmon said. "He'll have to prove himself in a hard environment where there is no mercy. He's got the intelligence and the tools to succeed very quickly. My only worry is that he's losing two of the best years of his life to do something that is very demanding for a young person. Considering everything, he's making the right decision, but he's going to have to grow up faster than I'd like him to."

Then came Tiger's great run for a third straight United States Amateur title, when he defeated Steve Scott in sudden death to make amateur golf history. And nearly everyone in attendance knew they were seeing Tiger Woods as an amateur for the last time. It was announced immediately after the tournament that Tiger would hold a major news conference that Wednesday, just forty-eight hours later. That was one day before the opening round of the PGA Greater Milwaukee Open. Speculation was that Tiger would turn pro and play in Milwaukee the very next day.

Tiger made his announcement on Wednesday, August 28, 1996. He explained how he had come to his decision. "I had intended to stay in school, play four years at Stanford and get my degree," he said. "But things change. I didn't know my game was going to progress to this point. It got harder to get motivated for college matches, and since I accomplished my goal of winning the NCAA, it was going to get harder still. Finally, winning the third Amateur in a row is a great way to go out. I always said I would know when it was time, and now is the time."

Despite Tiger's confidence in his decision, he felt bad about leaving school. He had promised both his parents and himself that he would get his college degree. He vowed to make good on that promise one day.

As predicted, he was entered in the Greater Milwaukee Open, which would begin the next day. What no one expected was the media hype and the excitement that was created by Tiger's announcement. Suddenly, he was more than a fine young golfer. As soon as he turned pro, there was a Tiger Woods frenzy that

Holding his father's hand for support, Tiger announces that he will not return to Stanford University, but will become a full-time professional golfer. The announcement caused a stir of anticipation throughout the sports world.

transcended the sports world. It seemed as if Tiger had become a national celebrity overnight.

Tiger's father and his representatives had known of his decision beforehand. They immediately got busy talking to various companies that might want

Tiger to represent them. That's when they learned just how valuable Tiger already was to many major companies. They saw Tiger as a pioneer in his sport as well as an outstanding athlete and golfer who would probably become a big winner.

At the time Tiger announced he would become a pro, Jim Thorpe was the only other African American golfer on the Tour. Though a fine pro, Thorpe was not among the golfing elite. Tiger, everyone felt, had a chance to be the best. In addition, he was young, good-looking, and very intelligent. He had the total package to become a multimedia star.

It was announced almost immediately that Tiger had signed two endorsement deals. One was with Nike, the shoe manufacturer, the other with the golf company Titleist. That wasn't surprising. It was the numbers that were. The two multiyear deals were said to be worth between $40 and $60 million. Tiger was an instant millionaire many times over.

Nike, for one, was betting that Tiger had the same kind of widespread appeal as basketball superstar Michael Jordan. Though Tiger was moving into a sport that was almost all white and not played by many young people, it was felt that his appeal would be universal, and that he would revolutionize the sport. PGA Commissioner Tim Finchem was one who fully believed in what Tiger could contribute to the sport.

"It is conceivable that in terms of overall impact on the sport," Finchem said, "when you figure in media, the dollars on the table for him, his ability to be a role model—that if he succeeds he might be the most important player ever."

Tiger's lawyer, John Merchant, felt one reason for all the excitement was Tiger himself and the way he had been raised. "Other athletes who have risen to this level just didn't have this kind of guidance," Merchant said. "With a father and mother like Tiger's, he *has* to be real. It's such a rare quality in celebrities nowadays. But watch Tiger. He *has* it. He actually listens to people when they stop him in an airport. He looks them in the eye. I can't ever envision Tiger Woods selling his autograph [a common practice among athletes today]."

Tiger himself was confident that he wouldn't be overwhelmed by the demands for his time and the commitments he had made. "I know I can handle all this," he said, "no matter how big it gets. I grew up in the media's eye, but I was taught never to lose sight of where I came from. Athletes aren't as gentlemanly as they used to be. I don't like that change. I like the idea of being a role model. It's an honor. People took time to help me as a kid, and they impacted my life. I want to do the same for kids."

Everyone predicted that Tiger would have a huge impact on the sport of golf. He was already known the world over. Practicing for the Masters in April 1996, he swapped shots with golfing legends Arnold Palmer (left) and Jack Nicklaus (center). They and other pros already knew how good Tiger could be.

Tiger knew that might not be easy because of the sport he played. Golf simply wasn't highly popular among young kids. But he was already making plans to change that.

"I just want to do my part," he said, "trying to help out as much as I can. As long as I can touch one person, I feel I've done my job. But I'm definitely going to try to do a whole lot more than that."

THE PRO TOUR

For Tiger to do some of the things he wanted to do off the golf course, he knew he'd have to excel *on* it. But that was the part he enjoyed more than anything. Despite the pressure and the tiring grind involved in winning a third straight United States Amateur tournament, he looked forward to playing again.

"Golf, to me, is like a drug," he explained. "If I don't have it, I go crazy. It's gone beyond love and hate. I always tell people I'm addicted. I've got to keep playing."

So Tiger traveled to Milwaukee, where he would join 155 other pros for the Greater Milwaukee Open. He was accompanied by his mother and father, as well as a number of other support people, a publicist, and several members of the management firm representing him. It was apparent which golfer the large galleries of fans had come to see. ESPN was covering the event for television, and the announcer opened the telecast by saying: "We are here for one reason and one reason only."

That reason was Tiger Woods. All eyes were on him as he stepped to the tee for his first shot as a professional. Tiger took out his driver and blasted the ball 336 yards (307 meters) straight down the fairway. A buzz went through the crowd. Those who had never seen him play before couldn't believe that a slim youngster could hit a golf ball so far.

Tiger played a fine first round. He finished the eighteen holes with a score of 67, an outstanding score with which to start a pro career. He followed that with a 69, making the cut and qualifying for the final two rounds.

Fatigue finally caught up with him in the third round. He shot a 73, which put him well back in the pack. He finished strong with a 68 for a total score of 277. He was seven under par for the tournament, but finished in a tie for sixtieth place. And during the final round he got his first hole in one, on the 188-yard (172-meter) fourteenth hole. The gallery went wild with excitement. His prize money was just $2,544. But he felt proud. He had earned it.

To his fellow pros, Tiger was impressive in every way. Loren Roberts, the winner of the tournament, shared the widely held belief that Tiger would be successful and good for the entire sport. "He's come along at exactly the right time," Roberts said. "He's like Arnold Palmer, a guy who is going to popularize the sport to a bigger audience, to reach out to areas where maybe golf has been slow to reach. He's got a lot on his shoulders. There's no question he's going to do well. When you hit your best shot and look up and he's sixty yards in front of you, that's impressive."

Veteran pro Bruce Lietzke was teamed with Tiger during the third round when he shot a 73. He saw a lot of Tiger's heart in that round. "I played with him on his bad day, nothing was working for him," Lietzke said, "and I was impressed. You learn about somebody when he's having that kind of day. A lot of twenty-

Tiger played well, but not great, in his first pro tournament, the Greater Milwaukee Open. Here, he blasts the ball out of a sand trap. In the background are hoards of fans, who seemed to follow him everywhere.

Tiger learned very quickly that he would always be the center of attention. Even in his first pro tournament the sportswriters, fans, and reporters were never far behind. Neither were their questions and their microphones.

year-olds would get frustrated, angry. He never lost his temper, still kept working. If he's going to be the game's next great ambassador, then the game is in good hands."

Tiger was happy to have that first pro tournament under his belt. It was already late in the golfing season. Tiger's plan was to play in six straight tournaments with the hope of winning enough prize money to get himself into the top 125 in winnings. If he did that, he would automatically qualify for all the Tour events in 1997. Otherwise, he would have to play in qualifying tournaments, which means extra rounds of golf.

In the eyes of many, his plan wouldn't be easy to realize. There were many comparisons to look at. Arnold Palmer and Jack Nicklaus were two of the greatest golfers ever, players who dominated their eras. Palmer had two top-ten finishes (including a tie for tenth) in his first seven tournaments, while Nicklaus was among the top-ten just once.

How long would it take Tiger to get there? His second tournament was the Bell Canadian Open, and he almost made it. He shot a 208 for the tournament, which was shortened to three rounds by bad weather, finishing eleventh. A week later he was entered in the Quad City Classic. There, he shot a 69-64-67 for the first three rounds and was in the lead going into the final eighteen holes.

Knowing Tiger as a strong finisher, many felt he would win. But there was one disastrous hole. It was a par 4, but Tiger suddenly couldn't find the cup and took four putts to finish. He had an 8 for the hole and finished the day with a 72, which dropped him into a tie for fifth place. Still, it was his first top-ten finish and just his third pro tournament.

A week later he did even better, finishing in a tie for third place at the British Columbia Open. He seemed to be getting closer. But after two tournaments, Tiger was exhausted. He was scheduled to play at the Buick Challenge in Pine Mountain, Georgia, the following week, then attend the Fred Haskins Award dinner, where he would be honored as the top collegiate golfer. Citing his hectic schedule, Tiger abruptly canceled his appearance at both. He didn't expect the criticism that followed this announcement.

Suddenly, fellow pros were jumping down his throat. They said that a professional golfer had to learn to honor his commitments. Some wondered if Tiger had taken on too much at too young an age.

Top pro Curtis Strange called Tiger "ungrateful" for turning down an invitation that was extended to him in order to help him get into the routine of the pro Tour as quickly as possible. The legendary Arnold Palmer also took his young friend to task.

"Tiger should have played," said Palmer. "He should have gone to the dinner. You don't make commitments you can't fulfill unless you are on your deathbed, and I don't believe he was."

It didn't stop there. Pro Tom Kite showed his skepticism when he said, "I can't ever remember being tired when I was twenty," while Peter Jacobson added, "You can't compare Tiger to Nicklaus and Palmer anymore, because they never [walked out]."

These reactions stunned Tiger. "I thought those people were my friends," he said.

What he didn't realize was that his life was now subject to everyone's scrutiny. Yes, he was expected to act like a professional. But the fact that Tiger was getting $40 million or more in endorsements probably made some others envious—most golfers get very few endorsement opportunities. Tiger quickly apologized to the tournament directors and sent letters of apology to all two hundred people who had planned to attend the Haskins dinner. Then he tried to put the incident behind him and concentrate on his next tournament, the Las Vegas Invitational.

TIGER WINS HIS FIRST

The Las Vegas Invitational was a big tournament, five rounds of eighteen holes each. There were always many celebrities from the entertainment and sports world on hand, as well as all the top pros. When Tiger shot a 70 in the opening round, it didn't look as if he had a chance to win. All the other golfers' scores were very low.

But in the second round his game began to come together. He shot a dazzling 63, the best round of his pro career. He followed with a 68 and 67 in rounds three and four. Going into the fifth and final round, Tiger was in a five-way tie for seventh place. There were still many golfers with a chance to win.

Despite a slight groin injury, Tiger was playing magnificent golf. As it became apparent that he was making a run at the leaders, the size of the crowd following him began to grow. Blasting off the tee, Tiger's shots traveled farther than those of any other golfer in the field.

Less than two months after turning pro, Tiger won his first tournament. He defeated Davis Love III in sudden death to take the Las Vegas Invitational. Here, a proud Tiger shows off the winner's check, to the tune of $297,000.

When Tiger sank his final putt on the eighteenth hole, he had shot a sensational 64 for the round and was tied for the lead with Davis Love III. Now the two golfers would play a sudden-death round for the championship. The first one to win a hole would win the tournament.

The two players returned to the eighteenth tee for the first hole of sudden death. Both got on the green and fairly close to the cup. Tiger sank his putt for a par, but Love missed a 6-foot (2-meter) putt and it was over. Tiger had won his first PGA tournament in just his fifth start.

"I'm surprised it took this long," said Tiger's coach, Butch Harmon. "I'm one of the few people who really knew how good he is. For him, to be able to just play golf was the key. He didn't have to go to school or do anything else."

Tiger didn't seem surprised by the win. Always supremely confident in his game, he said, "It [the victory] should have come at Quad City. I learned a lot from that."

Davis Love, who had just lost to Tiger in the play-off, summed up his feelings about the rookie pro, voicing the opinions of many in the golf world.

"He thinks about winning and nothing else," Love said. "I like the way he thinks. We were all trying to prolong the inevitable. We knew he was going to win. Everybody better watch out. He's going to be a force."

The victory brought Tiger into fortieth place on the money list, with $437,194 in prize money after five tournaments. He had achieved his goal of making the top money list, and was automatically qualified for one of the major championships, the 1997 Masters.

Following his victory at Las Vegas, Tiger had another chance to win. A third-round 73 slowed him, but he still finished in third place at the LaCantera, Texas, Open. A week later he was in Orlando, Florida, for the Walt Disney/Oldsmobile Classic. After shooting a fine 69 in the opening round, Tiger told his father, "Pop, I've got to shoot a 63 today. That's what it will take to get into [a position to win]."

Sure enough, Tiger played as if he were the only golfer on the course, exploding for a 63 in the second round to move up among the leaders. After a third round of 69, he was just one stroke off the lead. He played the final round in a group with veteran pro Payne Stewart. Both were on their game and contending for the championship. When it was over, Stewart had shot a fine round of 67. But Tiger went him one better, shooting a 66 for his second Tour victory. His four-day total of 267 was 21 under par for the tournament.

Tiger won another $216,000 for the victory, giving him nearly three quarters of a million dollars after just seven pro tournaments. Amazingly, Tiger claimed that he still wasn't playing as well as he could.

"I really haven't played my best golf yet," he said. "I haven't even had a great putting week yet."

Once again, his fellow pros were in awe of Tiger's immense talent. The great Jack Nicklaus, who had dominated an earlier era and was considered by many to be the greatest golfer ever, sang Tiger's praises to the hilt. "I don't think we've had a whole lot happen [in golf] in what, ten years," Nicklaus said. "I mean, some guys have come on and won a few tournaments, but nobody has sustained and dominated. I think we might have somebody now."

Some of Tiger's numbers were mind-boggling. For example, in his short time as a pro he already had twelve eagles. An eagle is achieved when a golfer completes a hole two shots under par. The Tour leader was Kelly Gibson. He had fourteen eagles. But it had taken him thirty-six tournaments to do it.

The average distance of Tiger's drive (his first shot off the tee) was 302.8 yards (277 meters). That was 14 yards (13 meters) better than runner-up John Daly. Tiger's scoring average as a pro was 67.89 shots per round. If he had enough tournaments to qualify, that would have been a new record. Greg Norman held the record for a full year at 68.81 shots per round.

Another longtime pro, Jay Haas, didn't mince words about Tiger's accomplishments. When asked, he called Tiger "the best player on the Tour."

A NEW ERA IN GOLF

Great golf wasn't the only thing that Tiger Woods was bringing to his sport. In the space of just a few short months he was already changing the face of the game. When he won his second tournament at the Walt Disney/Oldsmobile Classic, the galleries were more than three times their normal size. There were more young people and more minorities watching the matches. And they were there to see just one person—Tiger Woods.

Tiger was very aware of what was happening. He seemed to be enjoying every moment of it. "To look out here and see so many kids, I think that's wonderful," he said. "They see someone they can relate to, me being so young. It's really nice seeing more minorities in the gallery. I think that's where the game should go and will go."

On the course, Tiger often stopped to high-five his fans and responded when they cheered for him by thanking them for their support. He also threw extra golf balls to his fans in the gallery. Fans were turning out in droves to see, touch, and root for Tiger Woods.

"I remember when I was a kid," Tiger said. "I always wanted to be part of it [golf]. I always wanted to be connected somehow."

Working with kids is one of Tiger's favorite pastimes. He has started the Tiger Woods Foundation to promote his sport and to support charitable programs for youth in the inner cities. Here, he helps a youngster with his golf swing during a clinic in Lake Buena Vista, Florida, early in 1997.

Being a pro was demanding. Suddenly, his time wasn't his own. He still had to practice and play in tournaments. Everyone seemed to want him. In his spare time he had to do interviews, pose for photos, or perform in ads for his sponsors. He also missed college.

"I miss hanging out with my friends," he told a reporter. "I have to be so guarded now. There's no one my own age to hang out with . . . because everyone my age is in college. I'm a target for everybody now, and there's nothing I can do about it. My mother was right when she said that turning pro would take away my youth. But golfwise, there was nothing left for me in college."

It wasn't that Tiger regretted his decision to turn pro. He simply realized what he had left behind, and there were times when he missed that life. But his performance on the golf course and in the public eye more than proved that he was ready for the change.

Tiger finished 1996 in fine style. In eight pro tournaments, he had two wins, two third-place finishes, five top-ten finishes, and was in the top-twenty-five seven times. He ended the year with $790,594 in prize money, good for twenty-fourth place on the PGA list. He had done more than meet his goal.

Then, just before his twenty-first birthday, Tiger learned that he had been named "Sportsman of the Year" by *Sports Illustrated* magazine. In just four short months, he had risen to the top of the sports world. His name and face were already known worldwide.

The first Tour event of 1997 was the Mercedes Championships, held at the La Costa Resort and Spa in Carlsbad, California. All the top pros gathered once more, each hoping to get off to a good start in the new year. When it ended, the winner was once again Tiger Woods. This time he beat Tom Lehman for the championship. Lehman was the leading money winner in 1996 and the PGA Player of the Year.

Asked if he was surprised by his win, Tiger was once again open and honest without being cocky. "No. This is what I set out to do," he said.

Lehman, however, joined the growing ranks of veteran pros who didn't mind praising the new young superstar. "If I go out and play well and lose, I'm going to know there's a new kid on the block who's just way better than everybody else," he said, before the start of the final round. "Tom Lehman is the player of the year, but Tiger Woods is probably the player of the next two decades."

Visiting his mother's home country of Thailand in February 1997, Tiger played in and won the Asian Honda Classic. Kultida Woods holds a bouquet of flowers, while her son shows off the championship trophy.

Ernie Els, who had set a PGA record by winning $1 million in prize money in his first twenty-eight tournaments, watched as Tiger smashed his record. Tiger had just earned $1 million in a mere nine tournaments.

"Tiger is stunning all of us," Els said.

Early in 1997, Tiger traveled to his mother's home country of Thailand, where he was treated as a national hero. Though exhausted from the heat and a busy schedule, he promptly won the tournament held there. He also played in

Australia before returning to the United States. It seemed that his fame would soon spread to every country where golf is played.

Despite his commitment to golf, Tiger demonstrated that his family still came first when he abandoned the Tour for several weeks to stay by the bedside of his father. Earl Woods needed open-heart surgery, and Tiger was not about to go back to golf until he was sure his father was well on the road to recovery.

After his heart surgery, Mr. Woods convinced Tiger to play in the nearby Nissan Open in Pacific Palisades, California. Tiger didn't win. He was still worried about his father. He skipped the Doral Open and with the Masters coming up soon, Tiger's fans wondered if he would be ready.

The Masters, played in Augusta, Georgia, is the first of the four major tournaments played each year. Tiger had played the Masters twice as an amateur, but didn't do well. And at the 1997 Masters, he started poorly. On the first nine holes of the tournament he shot a 40. That was four shots over par. Many thought he was already out of the running.

Tiger then realized that he had a flaw in his swing. "I was bringing the club almost parallel to the ground on my backswing," he said. "That was way too long for me. I knew I had to shorten the swing."

Amazingly, he corrected the flaw immediately. He then went out and shot an incredible 30 on the back nine. That gave him a two-under-par 70 for the first round. He was only three strokes behind the leader. And he continued to play excellent golf.

Tiger stayed up for the second round, shooting the tournament's best score, a 66. Now, Tiger had a three-stroke lead in the tourney. And he didn't waver. His last two rounds were completed with scores of 65 and 69. He finished with a tournament record 270 and had won the Masters by a record-breaking 12 strokes.

When it was over, Tiger hugged both his father and mother. Then he spotted Lee Elder, one of the first black pro golfers. He hugged Elder as well, saying,

The scoreboard tells it all. Tiger gets ready to hit his shot on the 15th hole during final-round play at the 1997 Masters.

"Thanks for making this possible."

Later, Tiger said, "This is something I've always dreamed of. [Winning the Masters] means a lot to myself and my family."

Everyone praised Tiger's achievement. All-time great Jack Nicklaus spoke for many golfers when he said that "Tiger's out there playing another game on a golf course he's going to own for a long time. I don't think I want to go back out and be twenty-one and compete with him."

No one, not even Tiger Woods, can win every week. He didn't win the United States Open or the British Open in 1997. But he is still the most feared golfer on the course. All the pros know he is capable of winning any tournament he enters. And he continues to play the game with a boyish enthusiasm that is often contagious.

Tiger also shows his enthusiasm for being a role model by working with the National Minority Golf Foundation, which is headed by his father and one of his father's friends. He has started his own foundation, which will involve sports psychologists going into underprivileged neighborhoods to instill in children, through golf, a greater sense of self-worth. Tiger will make appearances and conduct golf clinics on behalf of the foundation.

After donning the traditional green jacket of the Masters champion, Tiger took time to chat with veteran pro Lee Elder. In 1975, Elder became the first African-American golfer to play in the Masters.

In the meantime, Tiger continues to work at being the best golfer and the best person he can be. To do this, he tries to live by the lessons of his youth and the solid foundation his own parents built for him.

"People can say all kinds of things about me," Tiger has said, referring to his golf game and his ultimate place in the sport. "But it still comes down to one thing. I've still got to hit the shot. Me. Alone. That's what I must never forget."

TIGER WOODS: HIGHLIGHTS

1975 Born on December 30 in Cypress, California.

1976 At the age of eleven months, demonstrates a remarkable golf swing.

1981 Appears on television's *That's Incredible!*

1984 Wins his first junior world championship in San Diego, California.

1990 Shoots a 69 for eighteen holes while playing with twenty-one touring professionals at the Insurance Golf Classic in Fort Worth, Texas.

1991 Wins first United States Junior Amateur championship.

1993 Becomes first golfer to win three straight United States Junior Amateur titles.

1995 Captures National Collegiate Athletic Association (NCAA) championship.
Finishes in a tie for twenty-second place against the world's top professionals at the British Open.

1996 Becomes the first person to win three consecutive United States Amateur championships.
Turns pro in the Greater Milwaukee Open, sinking a hole in one and finishing in sixtieth place.
Wins first pro tournament, the Las Vegas Invitational, in his fifth start.
Wins the Walt Disney/Oldsmobile Classic in Orlando, Florida.
Named "Sportsman of the Year" by *Sports Illustrated.*

1997 Wins the Mercedes Championships in Carlsbad, California.
Becomes the youngest winner of the Masters in Augusta, Georgia, setting a tournament record with a four-round score of 270.

FIND OUT MORE

Deegan, Paul. *The Masters*. Mankato, MN: Creative Education, 1992.

Italia, Bob. *100 Unforgettable Moments in Pro Golf.* Minneapolis: Abdo & Daughters, 1996.

Jensen, Julie, and Peter Krause. *Beginning Golf.* Minneapolis: Lerner, 1995.

Krull, Kathleen. *Lives of the Athletes: Thrills, Spills (and What the Neighbors Thought)*. San Diego: Harcourt Brace, 1996.

Wilner, Barry. *Superstars of Women's Golf.* New York: Chelsea House, 1997.

How to write to Tiger Woods:

Tiger Woods
c/o International Management Group
One Erieview Plaza, Suite 1300
Cleveland, Ohio 44114

INDEX